Written by **Makida Arshi**

SHINING AS I AM

Illustrated by **Siddhant Jumde**

To the autistic children, whose unique minds light up the world in ways we are still learning to understand. To the parents, who love tirelessly and advocate endlessly. To the siblings and friends, whose patience, compassion, and support make all the difference. And to the caregivers, whose dedication and care offer strength and comfort every day. This book is for all of you, for your resilience, and for the safe world you're helping to create.

Published in association with
Bear With Us Productions

© 2025 Makida Arshi
Shining as I am

ISBN: 979-8-9870882-4-1

www.justbearwithus.com

Written by **Makida Arshi**

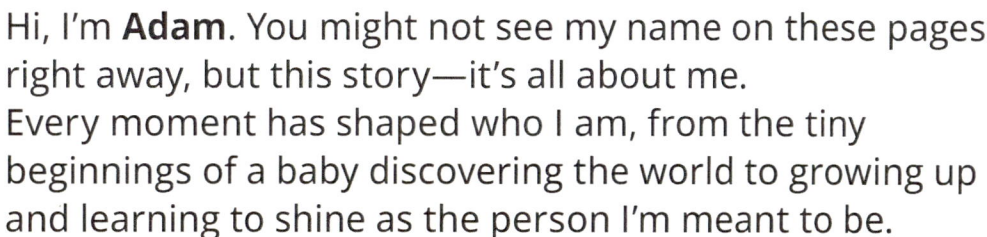

Hi, I'm **Adam**. You might not see my name on these pages right away, but this story—it's all about me.
Every moment has shaped who I am, from the tiny beginnings of a baby discovering the world to growing up and learning to shine as the person I'm meant to be.

But this isn't just my story—it's for anyone who's ever wondered if they're enough, if they'll find their way, or if they'll make a difference. I'm here to tell you: you will. Sometimes, it takes time to realise the light inside us.
So, let's start at the very beginning and realize how I found mine.

And when we reach the end, I hope you'll see some of your journey in mine, and you end up **'Shining As I Am!'**

Dear siblings and friends.

"Guess what? We've got exciting news,"
Said Mom and Dad one day.
"We're really pleased to let you know
A baby's on the way!"

The family was excited and
You jumped around in glee
To know that I would soon be there,
What fun you'd have with me!

You couldn't wait to welcome me
And get my nursery set.
For I was loved so very much
Before we'd even met.

So then I knew
You cared because
You truly loved me as I was.

Then finally the day arrived
When Mom gave birth to me.
Just like with you, the pain was great
(As childbirth can be).

The family gave support and love,
Were there to ease Mom's fears.
When I came into the world,
Everybody cheered!

Our parents were so happy and
Mom cried great tears of joy,
Holding me in her arms,
Kissing her newborn baby boy.

A newborn baby needs so much—
Warm baths and feeding too.
And changing diapers meant I gave
Our parents lots to do!

At times I found it hard to sleep
And cried into the night,
But Mom just whispered loving words
And held me oh-so tight.

So then I knew
They cared because
They truly loved me
As I was.

And then I crawled and took a step,
First milestones were done.
Mom and Dad were overjoyed
And so was everyone!

But as time passed, my progress slowed
In lots of different ways.
I was late in saying Mom and Dad,
I had a speech delay.

So then I knew
They cared because
They truly loved me
As I was.

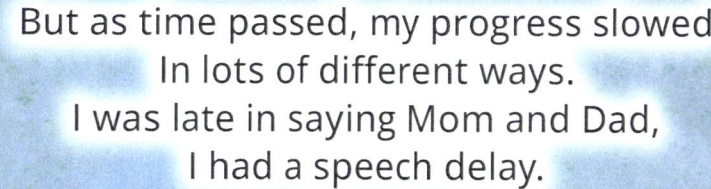

I found it very difficult
To look in people's eyes.
It made me feel uncomfortable,
Caused worries to arise.

Our family worried, but they knew
That patience was the key.
They never made me feel alone
Or stopped their love for me.

I didn't like loud noises or
The big sounds anymore.
No longer did I play with friends
Or siblings, like before.

I still knew
They cared because
They truly loved me
As I was.

We learnt to cope together
And took things day by day.
I understood things differently,
You loved me anyway.

The things that made us happy
Were as different as can be,
But you put in extra effort and
This means so much to me.

I sometimes like to hold onto
The things I really love.
When they capture my attention,
I cannot get enough!

But I'm adored for who I am
And who I'm meant to be.
Thank you for understanding and
For always loving me.

But I do know
And understand
You truly love me
As I am.

You've always loved me as I am
It makes me pleased inside.
I'm happy that you're here for me
And always on my side.

And I will be
Such a great man
Because you love me
As I am.

I sometimes rock for comfort,
It helps to calm me down.
At times I need to walk and walk
In circles all around.

And when I feel emotion,
Like sadness, joy or thrill,
I can't control my arms and it's
A challenge to stay still.

I may not tell you how I feel
Or know how you feel too.
I might not say just what I want
Or what I'd like to do.

I may cry for unknown reasons,
Am hard to reassure.
I struggle with my feelings and
I don't understand yours.

But when you take the time to care
And teach me what you know,
I can learn what feelings are
And what they mean and what they show.

I may need more attention
Than other people do.
I hope they're patient and kind
To my caregivers too.

I feel at home because
You understand
And truly love me
As I am.

I am a visual learner and
Like things that I can see.
I love my visual schedule that
My teacher made for me.

She writes what's happening on the board,
It makes me calm and so
If my daily routines change
The schedule lets me know.

And now I know
And understand
She truly loves me
As I am.

Elias likes to play alone,
He is my good classmate.
He doesn't say a word, but wow!
He plays piano great!

You celebrate my talents and
The things that I can do.
I'm very good at drawing and
It really calms me too.

Ahana is an awesome friend,
And when lunch is served at noon,
Ms. Chelsea helps her feed herself
And learn to hold a spoon.

We are AUTISTIC
And it's not something you can see,
But means we can feel overwhelmed—
Our brains works differently.

It's a spectrum that is varied,
Some might need great support,
Others just a little help
But always care and thought.

I hope people accept us as we are,
Are kind as they can be.
They'd be patient and would understand
If they knew what it means to me.

I want to feel that I belong,
That people can become my friend.
Just like them, I'm human too and
On others I depend.

Let your kindness and your patience
Be as gentle as can be,
It really means the world,
And I thank you for loving me.

And now I know
And understand

That I am loved and
SHINING AS I AM!

LOVE
FROM
ADAM

About the Author

Teaching children love, kindness, and compassion from a young age is vital for shaping a more empathetic and harmonious world. These values help children develop emotional intelligence, form healthy relationships, and understand the importance of caring for others.

By nurturing kindness and compassion early, we empower children to become thoughtful, respectful, and responsible individuals who positively impact their communities.

A loving foundation not only fosters their personal growth but also spreads warmth and understanding to everyone around them.

Makida Arshi